BUSH

CALIFORNIA

CALIFORNIA

Photography by WEST LIGHT

Craig Aurness   Brent Bear
Fukuhara Photography Inc.
Kenneth Garrett   Annie Griffiths
Pierre Kopp   Larry Lee
Charles O'Rear   Bill Ross
Steve Smith   Ralph Starkweather
Mark Stephenson and
William James Warren

The Golden State

Introduction and text by PETER JENSEN

BOULTON

©1985 Boulton Publishing Services, Inc., Toronto
Designed by Fortunato Aglialoro

ISBN 0-920831-00-1
1 2 3 4 – 7 6 5 4
Printed in Hong Kong by Scanner Art Services, Inc., Toronto

Introduction

This collection of photographs, ranging from snow banners 12,000 feet atop the Sierra Nevada to a child with her toes in the Pacific Ocean tides, did not happen overnight.

It happened one morning on Glacier Point in Yosemite shortly before daybreak, when the camera felt more like a cold chunk of metal than a magic paintbox. The sky was that certain deep field of blue just before the first bloom of sunrise; a dozen birdmen unfolded their nylon-and-aluminum wings to prepare for flight off the cliff edge. One photographer was there. Later that day a thousand would come and go from the point, but at that chilly, sleepy moment, only one was there.

It happened on a busy street in San Francisco as one figure broke the pedestrian pack and casually walked to the middle of the roadway, timing his crossing to focus on a lone cable-car against the sky. Only one of many passers-by stopped to compose a picture, jaywalking perhaps in doing so, but there to capture the moment.

It happened out on a desert highway, 30 miles from the nearest major road, maps spread across the dashboard, empty juice-cans piled next to the cooler in the back seat. Thirty miles of Joshua trees, washboard gravel-tracks, and rhyolite mountains. Light begins to change; eyes tingle with a new and wide band of vibrant colors. 'Stop the car!...'

Approaching a busy museum in Los Angeles, all eyes were on the building. Where was the entrance? How much a ticket? What was inside? Did sabre tooth tigers hunt on this site? Alone at an edge of the asphalt skirt, one photographer was down on his knee, wearing another hole in another pair of pants, shooting some striking yellow reflector-bumps lined up like egg yolks on the pavement.

Five o'clock in the morning once again. Los Angeles asleep. The photographer stands at the open window, feeling the cool, dry air flowing over the sill. A Santa Ana wind blowing off the desert drains the city's atmosphere of moisture, and the palm trees start to rattle. Within an hour, one shoulder bent under the weight of a camera bag large enough to hold a VW engine, the photographer has boarded a helicopter in Burbank for an aerial tour of the basin before the smog comes again; visibility clear from the San Gabriels to the Channel Islands. 'Unbelievable,' he mutters to himself as the motor-drive whirls along.

This is California seen through the lens, seen by eyes that watched every sunrise and sunset, every scudding squall and piled-high cumulo-nimbus. The look of California's sunlight, landscape, towns, and cities sets it apart. One could frame fifty photographs taken around the world, with only one from California, and Californians could probably pick that one without hesitation as being of *their* state alone.

The urge to describe and picture California in detail—throughout its history—has been without parallel. Today we approach moon shots and space walks with less enthusiasm to chronicle and observe than California's early visitors felt for their first glimpse of the green headlands above San Diego Bay.

'The next morning, which was Saturday, the fourteenth of March [1834], having a good breeze, we stood round the point, and, hauling our wind, brought the little harbor, which is rather the outlet of a small river, right before us. Everyone was desirous to get a view of the new place. A chain of high hills, beginning at the point (which was on our larboard hand coming in), protected the harbor on the north and west, and ran off into the interior, as far as the eye could reach. On the other sides the land was low and green, but without trees. The entrance is so narrow as to admit but one vessel at a time, the current swift, and the channel runs so near to a low, stony point that the ship's sides appeared almost to touch it.'

And so Richard Henry Dana, Jr., aboard *Pilgrim*, sailed into a channel that now regularly accommodates the aircraft carrier *Kitty Hawk*—with dozens of pleasure-craft to either side. Dana is probably coastal California's most-quoted author; his vivid journal *Two Years Before the Mast* was a great influence on Melville and generations of Easterners who dreamed of the sea and faraway places.

The vision of California as a land of bounty may have its origins lost in the mist of man's earliest times on the North American continent. The Spaniards certainly had a name for it: *El Dorado*, a fabled land of gold and spices. Surely entire Cities of Gold must wait to the north of the riches discovered by Cortez in Mexico! Pointing up the coast in the 16th century, their tiny galleons listing and rolling like walnut shells on a flood, fearful of storms waiting to drive them on uncharted shores, these Spaniards discovered instead a salubrious climate, lands rich in topsoil, kingdoms of trees, and bays swarming with clams, crabs, and fish.

Captains and crews seldom stayed longer than was needed to replenish fresh-water stores and go ashore in search of fresh fruits. Cabrillo in 1542. The Englishman Francis Drake in 1579. Sebastian Vizcaíno in 1602. But a theatre of wonder, a vision of a 'Magic Kingdom', had been discovered. Still, it was almost two centuries before Father Junípero Serra, 'Patron Saint of California', worked his way up on a string of missions in Baja California founded by Father Eusebio Francisco Kino to establish Mission San Diego de Alcalá in July of 1769. Over the next 54 years, 21 missions would be established along the California coast and through nearby inland valleys, each a stiff day's march apart.

El Dorado had taken on the golden hue of sunsets washing across adobe walls, of grains ripening and drying in valley fields under a hot California sun, of poppies drifting across the spring hillsides. Descriptions of the region, 150 years before the invention of color film, were suffused with this legendary glow. The first white men to come on foot to California continued past their Monterey Bay destination—they simply didn't recognize the spot so enthusiastically described by a journal writer on Sebastian Vizcaíno's expedition, just as busloads of tourists now prowl the streets of Hollywood, not seeing the Film Capital of the World beneath its streaked mascara, their questing fingers wearing smooth the concrete icons at the fabled Chinese Theatre founded nearly half a century ago by Sidney Grauman. On they go, hoping for a glimpse of an actor caught in the unlikely act of walking down a driveway to pick up the morning paper.

With golden glows came legends of opportunity. California overreached them all, for she delivered every time. Gold itself finally showed in the race at Sutter's Mill on a cold January morning in 1848. Within a year camps swelled along icy, bouldered Sierra rivers—men bent on 'trying their luck' poured into California by land and sea, and the population swelled to an astonishing 92,597. Only 20 years before, in the days of Mexican rebel leaders Pio Pico and Juan Bandini, settlers numbered 4,256.

The California dream, updated generation after generation, bound its people and their search for reaffirmation. Even in deep pain or failure, California stood ready to offer its magic balm. It might be nothing more than getting in a car and driving for miles, leaving the cities behind, following freeways that curved into mountains desolate and remote, and then plunged into valleys crosshatched by farms. Escape was there—in a walk beside the surf; on a high, dusty trail leading to snowfields in August; in canyons filled with the mist of waterfalls; on glaciated granite walls afire with sunset's alpenglow; or careening in a raucous schuss down a ski slope; or leaving the land, and worries, behind as you tuck into a wave at Will Rogers State Beach, feeling the monster suck on your toes and pull at your belly as you bodysurf into the curl.

With invigoration and renewal came a certain reclusive attitude. Californians were quick to recognize their riches, and eventually— unless they were land developers—hoped that others would stay away. Self-expression ran rampant, as Californians continued a tradition of breaking with the East Coast. They heard the Lord through McPherson's radio-tower-of-God, or sat in their cars at a drive-in theatre on Sunday. They sunbathed naked in San Diego's Balboa Park during an exposition marking the opening of the Panama Canal, while spectators lined the amphitheatre's rim. They marched 500,000 strong up Geary Street in San Francisco to protest an Asian war. They saw the musical soul of a generation and a city die at Altamont in the coastal mountains east of San Francisco. They built a sprawling city that hummed on eight cylinders, and ripped out the world's most extensive mass-transit system. Houses in chaparral hills looked like Normandy cottages, flying saucers, southwestern pueblos.

The split between North and South California widened. San Francisco was a prosperous world-port when Los Angeles was still a sleepy pueblo, and The City never got over its old-world attitudes toward an upstart southern sister. Both cities soon saw themselves as gateways to the Pacific Rim, rather than outposts of the Eastern Seaboard. The economic pendulum started its long, slow swing toward the west, gaining weight and momentum as orchards became centers of high-tech development and ports deepened to accommodate tanker-holds heavy with oil, Japanese automobiles, and redwood. El Dorado floated off over the horizon into the sunset, replaced by computer terminals blinking green spreadsheets.

To grow up in California is to be a tiny tycoon standing on a diving board above a money bin. A duck in your own Disneyland. The untold riches! Rafting on rivers wild with snow-melt. Skindiving in a Mendocino cove for abalone, then frying the pounded-thin steaks in butter over a campfire on the beach. Eating dinner each night for eighteen years in an Orinda house, watching the fog roll over the Berkeley hills in a tidal wave of slow-moving white.

The photographs here are windows on Californian memories. They don't glow with the hyperbole of early explorers, but with the reality of a state seen through ground glass. Some photographs took days to make. Some were the work of an instant of good fortune. This is the California we all long to see—and still can see, if we travel far and watch closely.

As I return from another trip to the California desert and sit at my desk in my house above the ocean, looking at these photographs, I reach into the bottom drawer for an old binder. There is a letter written in 1851 by my great-great uncle William Moore from the gold fields of California to his Wisconsin wife and children. Like everyone else in the family down to this day, he bragged about his cooking: 'We have had a feast today. Bought some dried peaches and I made two first-rate peach pies and baked bread, enough to last me all the week. I make light bread, none of your heavy stuff.' But there was hardship, and one wonders if he ever saw the golden California we see here in these pages.

Searching for gold along the Feather River, he 'traveled two days over snow, I should think it would average ten feet deep. On the second night it commenced snowing and such a snowstorm I never experienced before. I was forced to turn back, and then the trouble was to find and keep the trail. After three days of the hardest and most fatiguing time that I ever experienced I was fortunate enough to get out with my mule but had to throw away my baggage and provisions—all but my blankets. I knew I must stick to them or perish in the snow. There is nothing but good grit that will stand such storms as that, especially when men have to eat raw victuals and sleep in the snow. Oh, how often I think of you and wish I could be home...but this cannot be at the present for it does seem to me that I am doomed to leave my bones in California when I consider the luck that I have had while here, for I frequently see other men that have done well and seemingly without any effort on their part.'

There was an El Dorado, Uncle, if only your luck had held out. And there still is. These photographs prove it.

PETER JENSEN

1 *Monterey Parade of Elegance* Hood and radiator ornaments glint in the sunlight at Pebble Beach as the world's finest classic automobiles gather each year on the golf course for *concours* judging.   RALPH STARKWEATHER

2 *Hang glider and Half Dome, Yosemite* Five seconds after takeoff from Glacier Point, a pilot sets course toward balding Half Dome in California's famous national park. He'll soon swing left for the 3,000-foot descent to a landing point in El Capitan Meadow. Rangers grant flights only to world-class pilots, and only in the morning before 8 a.m. After that, thermal updrafts rise turbulently off the warming rock faces.   BILL ROSS

3 *Redwood National Park* Along the Pacific coast fogbelt from Monterey north into Oregon grows the magnificent coastal redwood *Sequoia sempervirens*. The coastal redwoods live for more than 2000 years. Growing to heights of more than 300 feet, *Sequoia* are the tallest trees in the world. BILL ROSS

4 *Santa Barbara Mission* Mirrored in a fountain that once laundered Indian garments, the 'Queen of the Missions' is the only one of California's 21 missions to have twin towers. Founded by Father Junípero Serra in the late 18th century, the chain of missions beginning in San Diego stretched north to San Francisco, each mission being set a hard day's march from the next. Their massive, classical architecture was constructed of adobe, rawhide-tied poles and clay roof-tiles curved over a man's thigh.

CRAIG AURNESS

5 (right) *Islets and 'sea stacks', Mendocino* Like teeth in a broken zipper of coastline, rock fragments were left behind in a relatively recent geologic uplift or isolated by the fierce pounding of waves. Skindivers brave the surf here in pursuit of abalone—a hand-sized mollusk that clings to grassy, underwater rocks.

RALPH STARKWEATHER

6 (left) *Santa Ynez Valley* Horsemen now consider this quiet valley northwest of Santa Barbara to be one of the finest breeding areas in the world, after Kentucky's Bluegrass Country.   CRAIG AURNESS

7 *Sunset, Santa Barbara Harbor* Mop-top palms line Cabrillo Boulevard in a city known for its red-tile roofs, Mediterranean architecture, and benign climate. Spaniards called it *La Tierra Adorado* (the beloved land), thanks in part to offshore islands that buffer the east-west coast from southern storms.   BILL ROSS

8 (left) *Yosemite*
Yosemite's great stone walls shoulder a winter storm. This view of the valley, a visitor's first upon leaving Wawona Tunnel, is surely one of the most photographed panoramas in the world. BILL ROSS

9 *Upper Yosemite Falls* The great naturalist and conservationist John Muir described the great falls' exuberant plumes as 'comets... At the top of the fall they seem to burst forth in irregular spurts from some grand, throbbing mountain heart.' Muir, 'against all reasonable judgement', once edged his way along a narrow shelf to the very edge of this 'pure wildness'. BILL ROSS

10 (left) *Tahoe pack station* Pony express riders once rode hell-for-leather across the Sierra passes west of Lake Tahoe. Today horses are more likely to tread peacefully on mountain trails, carrying campers and supplies to high-country camps.   CRAIG AURNESS

11 *Bodie in winter* A bitter snow muffles what was once one of the wildest gold-mining camps in the West. Sixty-five saloons bellied up to the dirt main street, and miners lost their wages to the girls of Maiden Lane and Virgin Alley. Today, ramshackle frame buildings, preserved in a state of 'arrested decay', are part of a State Historic Park.   ANNIE GRIFFITHS

12 *Mission Santa Inés* Named after St Agnes, the mission (1804) gave her name to the Santa Ynez Valley and was known for its extensive livestock herds and crops. Earthquakes, fires and other disasters damaged many of the California missions over the last two centuries; much of what can be viewed today is the result of extensive restoration work. BILL ROSS

13 (right) *Wildfire, Los Angeles* Rivers of fire fanned by hot, dry Santa Ana winds roaring through the mountain passes leap the ridgetops during Southern California's fall fire season. Most often caused by carelessness or arson, fires exuberantly consume the naturally thick, oily chaparral, endangering expensive homes and disregarding bulldozed firelines, until winds finally die.

CRAIG AURNESS

14 (left) *Sunrise, Tenaya Lake* 'Lake of the shining rocks', Tenaya's mirrored surface catches the morning's first rays at 8,150 feet elevation. Set in an arena of heavy glaciation, the lake is just north of Yosemite Valley on Tioga Road (State Highway 120).   BILL ROSS

15 *Napa Valley* A Californian who's never been on a horse is a bit like a Russian who's never tried Vodka. Here riders set out through the hot, inland valleys near Napa, north of San Francisco.   CHARLES O'REAR

16 (left) *Point Lobos State Reserve* Gateway to the Big Sur coast, Point Lobos digs into the sea with narrow blades of rock. Hikers follow paths through twisted cypress above deep cauldrons of waves and in winter catch glimpses of migrating gray whales rounding the Monterey peninsula. Poet Robinson Jeffers, who built his rock 'Tor House' here, wrote of these waves: 'White-maned, wide-throated, the heavy-shouldered children of the wind leap at the sea-cliff. The invisible falcon brooded on water and bred them in wide waste places, in a bridechamber wide to the stars' eyes in the center of the ocean...'   CRAIG AURNESS

17 *Hearst Castle, San Simeon* Architect Julia Morgan, California's first licensed woman architect, designed this 'castle' on the Central California coast for newspaper magnate William Randolph Hearst. Filled with European art and furniture, the home is a magnificently contrived blend of classical architectural fragments, Spanish renaissance, Beaux Arts styling, and inspired, original design. Now owned by the state and operated as a historic monument, it is one of the world's most-visited mansions: a true 'kingdom by the sea'.   CRAIG AURNESS

18 (left) *State Capitol, Sacramento* Renovated in the early 1980s, the 237-foot rotunda of the Capitol building (1861) no longer threatens collapse on the Legislature. California's capitol was moved several times before settling in this Central Valley city, gateway to the Sierra and gold country, and an inland port on the Sacramento River.   BILL ROSS

19 *Old Town, Sacramento* Tail lights streak the avenues of restored Old Town, once a ramshackle firetrap zone threatened with the wrecking ball. Now tourists clump along the boardwalks where Mother Lode miners looked to slake their thirst before booking passage on a riverboat to San Francisco.   CRAIG AURNESS

20 *Big Sur Highway, Central Coast* Closed in the early 1980s for more than a year by a huge landslide, the highway is a tenuous two-lane link between San Simeon and Carmel. Some call it 'the world's most beautiful drive', others fret over every hairpin curve above the thousand-foot drop. CRAIG AURNESS

21 (right) *North Coast dairy farm* Rustic farms stick to the high ground in the Eel River Valley between Loleta and Ferndale, south of Eureka. BILL ROSS

22 (left) *Sun-drying apricots, Santa Clara Valley* Pitted, halved sweet apricots spread like a sea of gold medallions near San Jose. Once the prune and apricot capital of America, the valley's orchards are now giving way to subdivisions. CHARLES O'REAR

23 *Future ketchup, California Delta* Tomatoes ride a conveyor to that big bottle in the sky. California's hot deep-soiled Central Valley, perhaps the world's richest agricultural region, spawned many a produce empire. Tall, earthen levees were built to reclaim delta 'peat land' from meandering Sacramento and San Joaquin rivers. CHARLES O'REAR

24 (left) *Panamint Valley mudflats* Furnace-hot in summer, Panamint Valley lies just west of Death Valley National Monument. Ancient lakes, left by a retreating ice age, once covered many of the California desert's valley floors.　WILLIAM JAMES WARREN

25 *Fort Ross, North Coast* Outpost for Russian fur hunters in the 19th century (during which California's and Oregon's great herds of sea otters were harpooned almost to extinction), Fort Ross sits on a grassy slope above the wind-chopped Pacific 13 miles north of Jenner. The little chapel was rebuilt in the 1970s after a devastating fire, retaining the wide, rough plank construction and vaulted ceilings so reminiscent of an inverted ship's hull.　CRAIG AURNESS

26 (left) *Sunrise from Glacier Point* Scratching the cold back of Half Dome, sunrise hits Glacier Point long before it spills down the Valley's vertical walls. Even at daybreak Yosemite is not quiet: from every canyon comes the constant roar and rock-clack of waterfalls.   BILL ROSS

27 *Regatta, Long Beach* Spinnakers set like musical notes along the horizon, 22-foot day sailors compete on an Olympic course near Pt. Fermin. Southern California's warm waters and steady winds make it a sailor's paradise.   PIERRE KOPP

28 *Date palms, Indio* Nurtured by artesian wells, some 200,000 date palms in the Coachella Valley thrive in a region that gets under 2 inches of rain a year. Algerian nomads might feel at home here but for a typically Southern Californian anomaly: oasis-side stands selling honey-sweet 'date shakes'.
BILL ROSS

29 (right) *Coastline, Laguna Beach* Time exposure creates an effect of misty scarves drawn through the rocks. Laguna Beach is a lively little Southern California community with dozens of art galleries and art fairs, elegant hotels such as the Surf and Sand, and scalloped beaches swarming with sunbathers. Underwater 'parks' beckon snorkelers and scuba divers.
CHARLES O'REAR

30 (left) *Kern River rafting, Southern Sierra Nevada* 'Hold on, we're going through!' shouts the oarsman, as this inflated pontoon raft hits a 'hole' in a Class V rapid on Kern Forks. He rows facing forward, levering the boat with long oars, trying for the mainstream. What degree of difficulty comes after 'Class V'? A waterfall: Class VI, generally considered unrunnable. BILL ROSS

31 *Vernal Falls, Yosemite* Slippery Mist Trail zigzags close to the wet tendrils of Vernal Falls (shown here in the decreased flow of late summer). Hikers can follow a cable handrail and trail to the falls' lip, where dark, cold water curves over a granite tongue, like bent steel. BILL ROSS

32 *Halloween pumpkins* The 'Golden State's' golden fall harvest: pumpkins by the millions. One of the state's most productive areas is Half Moon Bay, south of San Francisco.   FUKUHARA PHOTOGRAPHY INC.

33 (right) *Poppy field, Antelope Valley* Only an hour's drive from Los Angeles, the high desert's April carpet of wildflowers includes the magnificent state flower—the California poppy *(Eschscholtzia californica)*, preserved here in a state park near Lancaster.   BILL ROSS

34 *Laser research, Silicon Valley* On target: lasers split into spectral colors when they hit mirrors and a prism-like device set up by the technician. The area south of San Francisco, roughly between Palo Alto (home of Stanford University) and San Jose, has been dubbed Silicon Valley—a center of high-tech research for computer hardware and software based on the silicon microchip.

CHARLES O'REAR

35 (right) *Goldstone tracking station* Jet Propulsion Laboratory's Goldstone dish in the Mojave Desert monitors *Viking* and *Voyager* through deep space. California's space industry centers on Pasadena and JPL, Vandenburg (site of the new Shuttle pad), and Edwards Air Force Base (desert landing site for the Shuttle). WILLIAM JAMES WARREN

36 (left) *Steam vents, Lassen* Snowshoers trudge through deep snow in Northern California's Lassen Volcanic National Park to thermal areas near the park's south boundary. Lassen last erupted in 1915, uncorking a violent explosion that sent a plume of ash across North America. Today the park is one of the least discovered national parks. BILL ROSS

37 *Eastern Sierra near Mono Lake* Snow banners along the Sierra crest. Dry, light snow blows off the ridgeline near the Owens Valley aqueduct system—Los Angeles's long lifeline. CRAIG AURNESS

38 *Backyard docks, Newport Beach* A long way from Papeete, *Kim Long* noses up to her luxurious berth in Newport Beach. The houses may be only a few feet apart, but real estate prices routinely run in the millions. KENNETH GARRETT

39 (right) *Eagle Lake, Mineral King* Set in a glaciated cirque high above an alpine valley, Eagle Lake is typical of the high-country scenery found along the Sierra Crest. Mineral King, once the site of mining activity, is in Sequoia National Park. BILL ROSS

40 (left) *Vineyards, Salinas Valley* Sometimes called 'Steinbeck Country' (informally named for author John Steinbeck), the farmland running from Monterey deep inland along the Salinas Valley is rich in crops, including huge vineyards.   CRAIG AURNESS

41 *Bear Ranch, San Jose* Checking a fence on one of California's hundreds of working cattle ranches is still best done on horseback—especially when the spring mud is knee-deep.   BRENT BEAR

42 (left) *Lake Tahoe* Clear and icy-deep, Tahoe is 22 miles long and 8 to 12 miles wide between the California and Nevada sides. Roads wind 71 miles around its shoreline; here the view is west toward the Pacific Crest and Donner area. BILL ROSS

43 *Morro Bay* Putting the Montana de Oro coastline to its port side, a Morro Bay trawler heads out at first light for sea-bottom regions rich in lingcod and rockfish. BILL ROSS

44 *Stanford University* Palladian arches scallop one of the many courts and quads of the university founded in 1885 by Leland Stanford and his wife Jane as a memorial to their son Leland Stanford, Jr. Laid out on the founders' ranchland in Palo Alto, the campus was nicknamed 'The Farm'. The 1906 earthquake did extensive damage but the university quickly recovered and went on to develop its position as one of the leading academic institutions in America.   BILL ROSS

45 (right) *Delta agriculture* Plumes of peat dust cut across the stark geometry of a new field in the California delta.   CHARLES O'REAR

46 (left) *Newport Beach* California, where the land and the people greet the Pacific.
BILL ROSS

47 *Corona del Mar* Hull and sails burnished by sunset glow, a classic sailboat enters Newport Harbor with the hillside homes of Corona del Mar in the background.
RALPH STARKWEATHER

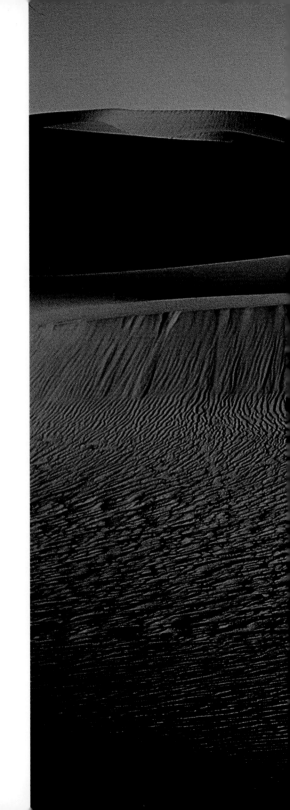

48 *Palm Springs* Reclaimed from desert sand, dozens of lush golf courses sprawl like green necklaces in the resort area. Many may exist chiefly to raise the real estate values of 'fairway homes', but many—especially the courses that wind back into the barren, rock-heap mountains—are serenely beautiful.

CHARLES O'REAR

49 (right) *Death Valley* Blown from ancient riverbeds and sinks, across a hundred miles or more, sand swirls to rest on ancient dunes near Stovepipe Wells. Temperatures here in winter are perfect for exploring the shifting, cupped formations.

BILL ROSS

50 *Palace of Fine Arts, San Francisco* Grandly European in scale and ornament, the Palace of Fine Arts was actually built as a temporary exhibition building for the Panama-Pacific International Exposition in 1915. Restored in 1967, it now houses the Exploratorium, a cavernous hall filled with hands-on scientific displays and inventions for children and adults alike. CRAIG AURNESS

51 *Mission San Diego de Alcalá* Founded by Fra Junípero Serra in 1769, this was the first of California's missions. Fire, earthquake and, in the last century, generations of neglect required several reconstructions of this graceful, white-washed church with its five-bell tower. The name is in honour of Saint Didacus of Alcalá in Spain, after whom the site of future San Diego had already been named by Vizcaíno in 1602. BILL ROSS

52 *Sunrise, Monterey Bay* Once known for its sardine fleet, Monterey has quieted with the mysterious disappearance decades ago of the small, silvery fish. Rickety 'Cannery Row' has mostly burned or gone 'boutique'. But the Mediterranean fishing legacy still thrives, especially with Sicilian squid fishermen who ply the night waters for cephalopods drawn to bright floodlights hung from trawler masts. CRAIG AURNESS

53 *Gold Rush Country* Mark Twain immortalized Angels Camp with his whimsical story *The Celebrated Jumping Frog*—a contest still held today. The big bulls can leap 10 or more feet. Betting was hot and heavy: 'I'll resk forty dollars that he can outjump any frog in Calaveras county,' boasted one character. Payments were often made in gold dust or nuggets found in the nearby, swift-flowing rivers.   BILL ROSS

54 (left) *Merced River, Yosemite* Fall color paints the valley floor along the Merced River's quiet bends and riffles. Though water levels are low and the great falls quieter, many visitors find that this is the park's most beautiful time of year. Steller's jays send their raucous cries down from the treetops, and campfire smoke hangs in the cool, still air. BILL ROSS

55 *Sequoia Big Trees in winter* Cross-country skiers trek between the massive, reddish-brown trunks of *Sequoia gigantea* that can reach 300 feet tall in maturity. Some are 3,000 years old. Their habitat is only a narrow range on the western slope of the Sierra Nevada. BILL ROSS

56 *Santa Monica Pier* Built when Santa Monica entertained hopes of being a significant port, the pier eventually became a haven for fishermen hoping to hook a big halibut, 'party' boats filled with anglers, and amusement park patrons. A classic merry-go-round still spins above the waves.   STEVE SMITH

57 (right) *Solvang* Danish immigrants built this Santa Ynez Valley town on nostalgic memories of butter cookies, handcrafts, and a farming tradition. Today the tourists pull off the highway for much of the same.
                                    CRAIG AURNESS

58 *Sleeping Beauty's Castle, Disneyland* Perhaps the best-loved and most-photographed sight in Disneyland park. Opened on 160 acres in 1955 to immediate success, and since much enlarged, Disneyland was the brainchild of the late genius Walt Disney, who had the simple but visionary idea of combining the fun of an amusement park with the setting and fantasies of films. Although widely imitated in America and abroad, Disneyland remains after 30 years the supreme original, with well over 11 million visitors a year.   BILL ROSS ©WALT DISNEY PRODUCTIONS

59 *Parachute tower, Knott's Berry Farm* It all began because Mrs Cordelia Knott's chicken dinners proved irresistible. When the Depression came to their Buena Park farm and berry patch, Cordelia and Walter Knott started selling pies and preserves at a roadside stand, then chicken dinners. Soon the line-ups were so long that Walter built a 'Ghost Town' to entertain the waiting customers. Today the 135-acre theme park sells over a million chicken dinners a year, and thrill-seekers try rides like this 200-foot parachute drop. BILL ROSS

60 (left) *Lompoc Valley flower fields* Half the flower seeds grown in the world are produced near Santa Barbara. Rainbows of calendulas, larkspurs, nasturtiums, poppies, and dozens more varieties bloom through the summer. CRAIG AURNESS

61 *Summer Olympics, Los Angeles* Bodies shaved, Lycra suits skin-tight, the world's top freestyle swimmers pierce the still blue pool during 1984 competition. Ridged design of lane-divider buoys cuts wave chop. BILL ROSS

62 *Beach volleyball* A unique Southern California adaptation to one of the world's most popular sports, beach volleyball is usually played with only two players to a side. Exhausting championship games can go on for three or more hours. Players serve, 'bump' (receive the serve off their forearms), set, spike (a rocketing hit across the net), and 'dig'—often a spectacular diving save in the soft sand. CRAIG AURNESS

63 (right) *Pismo Beach* Giant dunes, piled by wave and wind action south of the Central California town of Pismo Beach, are an open playground for motorists. Three-wheel, balloon tire motorcycles scramble like mad beetles. Buggy-whip antennas and flags announce their presence as they roar 'blind' over ridgetops. CRAIG AURNESS

64 *Night skiing, San Gabriel Mountains* Los Angelenos can drive to local mountain resorts in an hour, and operators extend the short season with snow-making machines and night lighting. In summer, the San Gabriels and San Jacinto ranges are welcome alpine respites above the great basin of smog.

BILL ROSS

65 (right) *Mono Lake tufa pinnacles* Bubbling springs, once underwater, formed these mysterious towers of mineral deposits. Mono Lake continues to grow more saline as water levels drop—waters diverted to a thirsty Southern California—endangering vast bird populations and brine shrimp. CRAIG AURNESS

66 *South San Francisco Bay* San Jose, Santa Clara, and the San Francisco Peninsula spread around the bay like a silicon computer chip. High-tech industries have turned the area into a clean-industry boom-town. CHARLES O'REAR

67 (right) *Badwater, Death Valley* Lowest point in the Western Hemi-sphere (282 feet below sea level), salt-encrusted flats catch enough winter rain to mirror the snowy Panamint Range. CHARLES O'REAR

68 (left) *Point Reyes* Protected as a National Seashore, Point Reyes juts into the sea in a barbed-fishhook shape just north of San Francisco. The wind here is relentless, yet wildflowers and grasses thrive on the salty bluffs and in the hillocks behind the drift-wood-littered beaches. BILL ROSS

69 *California poppies* (Eschscholtzia californica) *The State Flower* Spring's showiest flowers range from yellow to deep orange, and close each evening or when buffeted by desert breezes. On a clear, calm day the hidden, golden rivers of flowers pour off the hillsides. By May, the desert is barren again, and temperatures top 100 degrees. BILL ROSS

70 *Orange County groves* Still a major producer of citrus crops despite advancing new communities, Orange County blooms with the heady, sweet smell of Valencias and navel oranges. Artistic orange crate labels at the turn of the century helped promote Southern California communities like Valencia, Anaheim, Fullerton, Garden Grove, Whittier and (what else?) Orange. BILL ROSS

71 (right) *Golden Gate Bridge, San Francisco* Seen from Lincoln Park, the Golden Gate strides almost 6,500 feet through strong tides and foggy breezes running between the Marin headlands and Fort Point. Pedestrians and bicyclists can walk or pedal along the roadway's east side, 220 feet above the water. Twin towers anchor the impressive structure, connected by two transverse cables, each more than a yard in diameter, from which vertical cables hang like harpstrings. Completion was in May, 1937, at a cost of $35,500,000. MARK STEPHENSON

72 *Horse ranch, Central California* White fences stitch the range at a Santa Ynez stud farm, where classic, tawny, California hillsides rise in the background.   CRAIG AURNESS

73 (right) *Coastal foothills* Oak trees, solitary or in copses, spread their thick-limbed umbrellas over the dry coastal grasslands and gravelly hillsides.   CRAIG AURNESS

74 *Conifer forest, Yosemite* Forests of wonderfully varied conifers belt the Sierra, including huge sugar pines (over 200 feet tall), silver pines, Douglas spruce and fir, incense cedar, silver firs, two-leaved pines, mountain pines, Western juniper, mountain hemlock, and whitebark and nut pines. BILL ROSS

75 (right) *Surfer, Huntington Beach* With the curl fast closing ahead of him, a surfer drops down into a wave at one of Southern California's most popular surfing beaches. One move favored here is to 'shoot the pier'—that is to ride a wave between the pier pilings. PIERRE KOPP

76 (left) *Delivery, Anaheim stadium* California Angels play out of 'The Big A'—70,000-seat Anaheim stadium.   PIERRE KOPP

77 *Berkeley and Oakland* High in the Berkeley Hills, popular viewpoints along Skyline Drive look down on nuclear research facilities at Lawrence Laboratory (with its landmark rotunda-like building) and the bay beyond.   BILL ROSS

78 (left) *Theme restaurant, LAX* Los Angeles International Airport's Theme Building appears ready to stride with spider steps across nearby runways. A circular restaurant lets diners look across terminals to taxiing jets. Recently expanded to a second level for the Olympics, busy LAX is seldom overwhelmed by travelers and traffic.   PIERRE KOPP

79 *Page Museum, La Brea Tar Pits* Airy space-frame of the George C. Page Museum of Paleontological Discoveries (opened 1977) is bounded on four sides by a cast frieze depicting what the La Brea area (now Wilshire Boulevard in Los Angeles) may have looked like during an era of mastodons and sabre-tooth cats. Drawn to the tar pits by clear water floating over thick tars, animals blundered into the ooze and sank, their bones well preserved in the airless sludge.

FUKUHARA PHOTOGRAPHY INC.

80 (left) *Carmel Highlands* Private kingdoms carve out homesites along the Carmel coast, claiming rocky inlets and small bays as their backyards. Often the homes are marked by nothing more than a narrow drive leading off Highway 1.   CRAIG AURNESS

81 *Lone Cypress, Monterey Peninsula* A wind-shaped 'bonsai', famous Lone Cypress sends its roots into an outcrop's hairline fissures along scenic 17-Mile Drive. Six golf courses wind through the forest and along the ocean's edge in Del Monte Forest, including world-famous Pebble Beach.   CRAIG AURNESS

82 (left) *Dana Meadow, Tioga Pass* Alpine meadows in the Sierra Nevada were once lakes trapped in granite. Over thousands of years, decaying organic matter has gradually reduced the lake's depth until grasses, wildflowers, and eventually trees can take hold in the bog.   BILL ROSS

83 *Emerald Bay, Lake Tahoe* Sternwheel sightseeing vessel takes a turn around Emerald Bay's tiny island, once probably the center of a volcanic bowl that collapsed, admitting Lake Tahoe's waters.   BILL ROSS

84 (left) *Edwards Mansion, Redlands* A postcard scene of turn-of-the-century Southern California, Edwards Mansion is now a restaurant set in the orange groves.   BILL ROSS

85 *Christian Brothers Winery, St Helena* Napa Valley vineyards, of cabernet sauvignon, pinot noir, chenin blanc, and many other varietals, thrive on hot summers, foggy mornings and fingers of ocean air that find their way deep into the valleys. Pickers move between the trellised vines, sent into action by winemakers who measure the precise sugar content of the crush.   CHARLES O'REAR

86 (left) *San Francisco, Old and New* The downtown skyline at night, seen from Steiner Street in the foreground.   CHARLES O'REAR

87 *Cable car, San Francisco* Running again after a two-year, multimillion-dollar refurbishing in the early 1980s, cable cars climb the hills, powered by constantly moving cables sunk in the streets. Brakemen inside the wood and glass cars tug and push on a series of levers to 'grip' the humming cable, all the time clanging their brass bells in distinctive, stacatto rhythms.   WILLIAM JAMES WARREN

88 *Los Angeles skyline at sunset* One of Los Angeles's many 'down-towns', the central area rose over two centuries on the site of El Pueblo, the original Spanish settlement founded in 1781 to secure Spain's tenuous hold on Alta California. For decades during LA's mid-20th century growth the distinctive City Hall tower (third large building from the right) was the only tall building allowed by city ordinances as being able to brave the earthquake tremors. CRAIG AURNESS

89 *The* Star of India *Maritime Museum, San Diego* The masts of this
square-rigged old lumber-schooner turn into San Diego's largest
Christmas tree each holiday season.   BILL ROSS

90 Queen Mary, *Long Beach* Looking almost stubby to the telephoto lens, she was once the largest and fastest passenger vessel afloat, a high-seas palace of glittering crystal, heavy silver settings, and luxurious drawing rooms. She carried three-quarters of a million troops during *World War II* back and forth across the Atlantic, eluding 'wolf packs' with her 28-knot speed. PIERRE KOPP

91 (right) *Telegraph Hill, San Francisco* Night falls on Coit Tower and Columbus Avenue and the Church of Saint Peter and Saint Paul. LARRY LEE

92 (left) *Mt Whitney* Cleaved by geologic forces that turned much of the Eastern Sierra Nevada into a precipitous wall rising from the Owens Valley, 14,496-foot Mt Whitney stands more as a highpoint in the crest than as a single mountain.   CHARLES O'REAR

93 *Lake Castaic* Unlikely in an arid land, Lake Castaic is part of the Los Angeles water system—a terminus for Sierra Nevada and Central Valley waters. Stiff winds through the Gorman area make it ideal for high-performance day-sailing.   LARRY LEE

94 *Opening Ceremonies, Los Angeles Olympics, 1984* Produced like the best of Hollywood musicals, the Olympics opened with thousands of choral voices filling Los Angeles Coliseum.   BILL ROSS

95 *Olympic steeplechase, Los Angeles, 1984* Steeplechase runners are
caught silhouetted against the Coliseum scoreboard.   BILL ROSS

96 *Manns' Chinese Theatre, Los Angeles* Founded by Sidney Grauman in 1927, this opulent movie-house has been the setting of countless Hollywood premieres and is famous for its mementoes of movie stars.

BILL ROSS

97 (right) *San Francisco by night* The Financial District with the Transamerica Building seen from Coit Tower.

MARK STEPHENSON

98 (left) *Sunrise over Santa Monica* Still clear beneath a low cloudcover, Los Angeles Basin usually fills by midday with a pall of smog trapped by a lid of warm air and surrounding mountain ranges.
RALPH STARKWEATHER

99 *Aground on Monterey Peninsula* Off course in a thick fog, a sailboat waits for a high tide and rescue. Sailors who leave the relative sanctuary of Monterey Bay to view the beautiful rocky coast risk a confusing trip home through unexpected fogbanks.
CRAIG AURNESS

100 (left) *Avalon Harbor, Catalina Island* Tiny Avalon swells each day with tourists who make the 21-mile sail over from Long Beach on daytrip boats. At night, the town settles into a quieter pace as boaters, anchored in the crowded harbor, come ashore for dinner or a movie at the grand turreted Casino. But for the town, most of the island is uninhabited. RALPH STARKWEATHER

101 *First frost, maple leaves* A light freeze dusts the edges of maple leaves, already beginning their slow return to the soil. BILL ROSS

102 *Pfeiffer Beach, Big Sur* Waves undercut rock with the explosive force of water and air driven into cracks, battering a 'door' open in this hunched seastack off the Big Sur coast. Now swells roll freely to a quiet, moody beach behind the brooding silhouette.   CRAIG AURNESS

103 (right) *Closing ceremonies, Los Angeles Olympics, 1984* Like fireflies on the stadium walls, spectators shine their flashlights into the night sky, waiting the arrival of a 'UFO' during spectacular closing ceremonies.   BILL ROSS

104 *Joshua tree, Mojave Desert* A sentinel of the high desert stands watch as the sun goes down over California.   BILL ROSS